Turning Hopeless Situations Around

Kenneth E. Hagin

Unless otherwise indicated, all Scripture quotations in this volume are from the *King James Version* of the Bible.

Fifteenth Printing 1995

ISBN 0-89276-022-2

In the U.S. write:	In Canada write:
Kenneth Hagin Ministries	Kenneth Hagin Ministries
P.O. Box 50126	P.O. Box 335, Station D,
Tulsa, OK 74150-0126	Etobicoke (Toronto), Ontario
	Canada, M9A 4X3

BOOKS BY KENNETH E. HAGIN

* Redeemed From Poverty, Sickness and Spiritual Death
* What Faith Is
* Seven Vital Steps To Receiving the Holy Spirit
* Right and Wrong Thinking
  Prayer Secrets
* Authority of the Believer (foreign only)
* How To Turn Your Faith Loose
  The Key to Scriptural Healing
  Praying To Get Results
  The Present-Day Ministry of Jesus Christ
  The Gift of Prophecy
  Healing Belongs to Us
  The Real Faith
  How You Can Know the Will of God
  Man on Three Dimensions
  The Human Spirit
  Turning Hopeless Situations Around
  Casting Your Cares Upon the Lord
  Seven Steps for Judging Prophecy
* The Interceding Christian
  Faith Food for Autumn
* Faith Food for Winter
  Faith Food for Spring
  Faith Food for Summer
* New Thresholds of Faith
* Prevailing Prayer to Peace
* Concerning Spiritual Gifts
  Bible Faith Study Course
  Bible Prayer Study Course
  The Holy Spirit and His Gifts
* The Ministry Gifts (Study Guide)
  Seven Things You Should Know About Divine Healing
  El Shaddai
  Zoe: The God-Kind of Life
  A Commonsense Guide to Fasting
  Must Christians Suffer?
  The Woman Question
  The Believer's Authority
  Ministering to Your Family
  What To Do When Faith Seems Weak and Victory Lost
  Growing Up, Spiritually
  Bodily Healing and the Atonement
  Exceedingly Growing Faith
  Understanding the Anointing
  I Believe in Visions
  Understanding How To Fight the Good Fight of Faith
  Plans, Purposes, and Pursuits
  How You Can Be Led by the Spirit of God
  A Fresh Anointing
  Classic Sermons
  He Gave Gifts Unto Men:
      A Biblical Perspective of Apostles, Prophets, and Pastors
  The Art of Prayer

Following God's Plan For Your Life
The Triumphant Church
The Price Is Not Greater Than God's Grace (Mrs. Oretha Hagin)

MINIBOOKS (A partial listing)

* *The New Birth*
* *Why Tongues?*
* *In Him*
* *God's Medicine*
* *You Can Have What You Say*
  How To Write Your Own Ticket With God
* *Don't Blame God*
* *Words*
  Plead Your Case
* *How To Keep Your Healing*
  The Bible Way To Receive the Holy Spirit
  I Went to Hell
  How To Walk in Love
  The Precious Blood of Jesus
* *Love Never Fails*
  Learning To Flow With the Spirit of God
  The Glory of God
  Hear and Be Healed
  Knowing What Belongs to Us
  Your Faith in God Will Work

BOOKS BY KENNETH HAGIN JR.

* *Man's Impossibility — God's Possibility*
  Because of Jesus
  How To Make the Dream God Gave You Come True
  The Life of Obedience
  God's Irresistible Word
  Healing: Forever Settled
  Don't Quit! Your Faith Will See You Through
  The Untapped Power in Praise
  Listen to Your Heart
  What Comes After Faith?

MINIBOOKS (A partial listing)

* *Faith Worketh by Love*
  Blueprint for Building Strong Faith
* *Seven Hindrances to Healing*
* *The Past Tense of God's Word*
  Faith Takes Back What the Devil's Stolen
  "The Prison Door Is Open — What Are You Still Doing Inside?"
  How To Be a Success in Life
  Get Acquainted With God
  Showdown With the Devil
  Unforgiveness
  Ministering to the Brokenhearted

*These titles are also available in Spanish. Information about other foreign translations of several of the above titles (i.e., Finnish, French, German, Indonesian, Polish, Russian, etc.) may be obtained by writing to: Kenneth Hagin Ministries, P.O. Box 50126, Tulsa, Oklahoma 74150-0126.

Contents

1. What Can You Believe? 1

2. What Do You See? 7

3. Plead Your Case 13

4. Correct Your Situation 17

5. A Favorite of the Father 21

6. Act Like It's True 25

Chapter 1
What Can You Believe?

The Lord is still in the healing business, saving business, and baptizing in the Holy Spirit business. Nothing is too hard for the Lord. Nothing is impossible with Him.

We think things are impossible, but with God nothing is impossible. If you can believe that, the impossible can happen in your life.

That's what Jesus said to the man who brought his son for healing. The son had some kind of spells. At times he would fall into water or fire. His father had his mind on what Jesus could do. He said, *"If thou canst DO any thing, have compassion on us, and help us"* (Mark 9:22).

That's where a lot of folks miss it. They've got their mind on "What can you do to help me?" But that's not the main problem at all. The main problem is: "What can you believe?"

Jesus answered the man, *"If thou canst believe, ALL THINGS ARE POSSIBLE TO HIM THAT BELIEVETH"* (Mark 9:23).

ALL things are possible! How many things? ALL. Say that out loud: "ALL THINGS ARE POSSIBLE." Say it again: "ALL THINGS ARE POSSIBLE." Say it again: "ALL THINGS ARE POSSIBLE."

To whom are they possible? To the person who believes. Say this out loud: "I BELIEVE."

Too frequently we look at situations and say, "That's impossible." We look at conditions and say, "That's impossible." But, praise God, *there is no such thing as an impossibility.* I don't care what it is. I don't care how hopeless and helpless it looks.

Somebody said, "We need to become *possibility*

1

thinkers." Too much of the time we're *impossibility* thinkers. We're trained to think that way. If you don't get your mind renewed with the Word of God — if you let your flesh dominate you — you'll keep on thinking that way until it is impossible. You'll say, "That's impossible."

We need to retrain our thinking. All things *are* possible. All things are possible to him that *believeth*.

This worked in Old Testament days, too. We can learn a great deal studying how God helped men and women in the Old Testament. We can see what these individuals did to obtain help. (You see, if God is the Healer under the Old Testament, He's the Healer under the New.) Some of the same principles work. After all, human nature is the same; it hasn't changed. It is identically the same. Human beings and human nature were the same under the Old Testament as they are under the New.

Sin is also the same. Disease and sickness are the same. A fellow who was stricken with leprosy in the Old Testament wasn't any different from one stricken with leprosy in the New Testament. And if a man stole something in Old Testament times, his sin was no different from that of the man who stole under the New Testament.

God is the same God now that He was then. He never changes. The Bible says He never changes.

Let's examine the case of King Hezekiah, an Old Testament figure who believed that all things are possible with God.

ISAIAH 38:1-3
1 In those days was Hezekiah sick unto death. And Isaiah the prophet the son of Amos came unto him, and said unto him, Thus saith the Lord, Set thine house in order: for thou shalt die, and not live.
2 Then Hezekiah turned his face toward the wall,

and prayed unto the Lord,
3   And said, Remember now, O Lord, I beseech thee,
how I have walked before thee in truth and with a
perfect heart, and have done that which is good in thy
sight. And Hezekiah wept sore.

Did you notice Hezekiah didn't say he had been perfect? Reading about him, we readily see he wasn't perfect.
But he said he had served God by walking "in truth and
with a perfect heart." And that's of utmost importance. His
heart was right toward God.

Many years ago I was holding a meeting in Kansas.
One afternoon I went to the church to prepare for the
evening service. I was praying, and I got to talking to the
Lord about the past. I could see some places where I had
missed it. At the time I thought I had done very well. But
when I looked back, I could see some glaring mistakes, and
I felt bad about them.

The Lord puts our mistakes under the blood when we
ask Him to. Not only that, He said He hides our sins in the
depths of the sea (Micah 7:19). And like Corrie ten Boom
said, we oughtn't to go fishing for them! But, being human,
we sometimes do.

So I was fishing for some of those things hidden in the
sea of God's forgetfulness — things that can affect your
faith and hinder you from obeying God and being an effec-
tive minister of the Gospel if you get to thinking about
them.

I remember how the Lord helped me that day. While I
was praying, the Lord reminded me of what He said the
time Samuel went down to Jesse's house to anoint one of
his sons king in Saul's stead. Samuel didn't know which
young man it was to be.

Naturally they brought the oldest son, Eliab, out first.

When Samuel saw him, he said — evidently to himself and maybe to the Lord — *"Surely the Lord's anointed is before him"* (1 Samuel 16:6). Eliab was of a beautiful countenance; he was of a fine stature. He must have looked like a king. *Surely it must be he,* Samuel thought.

It is strange how God selects some of the most unlikely prospects and makes kings out of them when they don't even look like kings. (You know, you're a king.)

The Lord said to Samuel, "He's not the one." He said, *"Look not on his countenance, or on the height of his stature; because I have refused him: for the Lord seeth not as man seeth; for man looketh on the outward appearance, but the Lord looketh on the heart"* (1 Samuel 16:7).

We're not the Lord. All we can see of a person is the outward appearance unless God gives us discerning of spirits to look into a human spirit. That's the reason we can't judge others. That's the reason the Bible says, *"Judge not, that ye be not judged"* (Matt. 7:1).

The Lord said to me, "I wasn't looking at you on the outside. You're looking at where you missed it from purely the physical, human, natural standpoint. But I was looking at your heart all the time. Your spirit is your heart. I saw the intent of your heart. Even though you had done wrong and had missed it, I wrote down, 'This man's heart is perfect toward me.' "

When the Lord said that to me, it was so real I began to weep in His presence. It did something on the inside of me.

We read where Hezekiah was reminding the Lord that his heart was perfect toward the Lord; he didn't say *he* always was perfect. But Hezekiah wanted to do the right thing, whether he did it or not. That's what the Lord is looking for.

Then the Bible says that Hezekiah "wept sore." That means with great weeping.

ISAIAH 38:4,5
4 Then came the word of the Lord to Isaiah, saying,
5 Go, and say to Hezekiah, Thus saith the Lord, the God of David thy father, I have heard thy prayer, I have seen thy tears: behold, I will add unto thy days fifteen years.

Notice He didn't just say, "I heard your prayer." He also said, "I've seen your tears."

To summarize, it says in the first verse that Hezekiah was "sick unto death." That means he was dying. Isaiah the prophet came and gave him a message from the Lord, saying, *"Set thine house in order: for thou shalt die, and not live."*

Not only was King Hezekiah incurably ill, but God Himself had pronounced a death sentence on him!

What is amazing is that Hezekiah did not die. Furthermore, he did not set his house in order. What did he do? Thank God, the Bible tells us exactly what he did: *"Then Hezekiah TURNED HIS FACE TOWARD THE WALL, and prayed unto the Lord"* (v. 2).

We know that Hezekiah also cried and prayed. All of us have cried and prayed at times, and it didn't get us results, so we know there has to be more to it than that. The other important fact is that Hezekiah turned his face to the wall. There's great significance to that.

What does it mean? *It means he turned away from man.* The reason many people haven't gotten results yet is because they're looking to man for results. Perhaps they're looking for some prophet to deliver them.

But Hezekiah not only turned away from man; he even

turned his face from Isaiah, who was the greatest of the prophets!

He turned his face away from his own sensations.

He turned his face away from his own symptoms.

He turned his face away from his own sufferings.

He turned his face away from sympathizing relatives.

He turned his face away from medical skill.

He turned his face to the wall.

And with his face to the wall, Hezekiah could only see one thing: God.

Chapter 2
What Do You See?

In the book *The Great Physician*,[1] which inspired this message, Dr. Lilian B. Yeomans told about a famous English preacher by the name of Dr. Joseph Parker, pastor of City Temple in London. As he was crossing the Atlantic by ship to minister in North America, some young men on board were anxious to meet him, because he was famous.

But Dr. Parker just sat on deck hour after hour, gazing at the vast expanse of water. He seemed unaware of anything around him.

Finally, one young man approached Dr. Parker and asked, "What do you see there?"

Dr. Parker replied without even turning his head, "Nothing but God. Nothing but God."

When you turn your face to the wall, you see nothing but God.

With his face to the wall, King Hezekiah saw nothing but God. And he cried unto God and prayed with tears.

And this God with whom nothing shall be impossible heard and answered that prayer!

Before Isaiah even got out of the palace courtyard, the Lord said to him, "Go back and announce to the king that I've heard his prayer and seen his tears, and his request is granted. I'm going to give him 15 more years. I'm going to add 15 years to his life." (It is possible that even more time was added later on.)

In all ages, those who have done exploits for God were those who turned their faces to the wall. By that I mean that they turned away from everything connected with

7

human reasoning and looked entirely to divine reasoning: to God and to Him alone. They got results.

In the beginning book of the Bible, Genesis, we see how Noah saved the human race from extinction by turning his face to the wall, so to speak. He found grace with the Lord, and was told to build an ark. That ark is a type of Christ, who is the Refuge of His people from judgment.

If people today would turn from everything else and turn to Christ, they would find that He is still the Refuge — and that the only safe place is really in Him.

That's the reason we shouldn't be disturbed about tidings of His Second Coming. Jesus told us all these things were coming. Jesus said there would be wars and rumors of wars, earthquakes, famines, and such things, with men's hearts failing them for fear for looking on the things that are coming to pass upon the earth.

When these things begin to come to pass, He said, *"then look up, and lift up your heads; for your redemption draweth nigh"* (Luke 21:28). Notice He didn't say "Run away and hide and stick your heads in the sand." He said, "Lift up your heads"!

I don't know about you, but I'm looking up and rejoicing, for our redemption "draweth nigh." We received part of our redemption and inheritance when our spirits were reborn. But thank God we're also going to have brand new bodies someday.

1 CORINTHIANS 15:52
52 In a moment, in the twinkling of an eye, at the last trump: for the trumpet shall sound, and the dead shall be raised incorruptible, and we shall be changed.

1 THESSALONIANS 4:16-18
16 For the Lord himself shall descend from heaven with a shout, with the voice of the archangel, and with

the trump of God: and the dead in Christ shall rise first:
17 Then we which are alive and remain shall be caught up together with them in the clouds to meet the Lord in the air: and so shall we ever be with the Lord.
18 Wherefore comfort one another with these words.

Isn't that a comfort?

So I'm not looking down; I'm looking up. Christ is still the Refuge. He's our Refuge from judgment!

Judgment is not coming on the Church. The Bible said if we would judge ourselves, we would not be judged (1 Cor. 11:31). That means, if we miss it, we just say, "I missed it. That's wrong. Forgive me" — and He forgives us.

For He said,*"For if we would judge ourselves, we should not be judged."* So judgment isn't coming on the Church.

I can't understand all these people running around hollering, "The Church is going through the Tribulation." The Tribulation is *judgment.* Is judgment coming on the Church? No. He said, "If you'll judge yourself, you'll not be judged."

Did the judgment come on Noah, his wife, and their family? No, the ark saved them from it. It was their refuge. That ark was a type of Christ. I have found refuge in Christ. Judgment is not coming upon me.

Why would the Church be judged and be under the same judgment of God as the rest of the world? It's utter foolishness to think so.

You can believe what you want to about it; that's still not going to change it. It's going to be just like the Bible says.

Jesus is coming. I'm looking up and rejoicing. You can

look down, complain, talk unbelief, and tell about how bad things are getting — but I'm telling you about how good things are and how much better they're going to be.

Again looking at an Old Testament example, when everybody had failed Moses, he turned his face to the wall. The children of Israel had turned away from God. They were worshipping the golden calf. God would have destroyed the nation if Moses had not stood in the breach to turn away His wrath.

Moses simply said, "Now, Lord, if You're going to blot their names out of Your book, just blot my name out along with theirs."

That means he turned his face to the wall. Moses wasn't seeing anything but God.

He wasn't seeing the golden calf. He wasn't seeing the failure of the people. He wasn't even seeing how his brother Aaron had failed him. He was seeing nothing but God.

The Lord said, "All right, I won't blot any of you out."

David at Ziklag is another Old Testament example of a man's turning his face to the wall. David's possessions were in ashes. His loved ones had been taken into captivity, and his followers, who were so noted for their loyalty, were ready to stone him. But thank God, David turned his face to the wall.

It says in First Samuel 30:6, *"but David encouraged himself in the Lord his God."* That means he turned his face to the wall. He saw nothing but God. The result was a great victory for David. He got his loved ones back and a great spoil besides.

History gives us even more examples, Dr. Yeomans points out. Augustine, the noted sixth century bishop, wrote about a high-ranking man of Carthage who was near death after a number of unsuccessful operations. He was facing yet another operation; however, his physicians had no hope it would be successful.

When Augustine arrived to pray for the nobleman, the man fell on the floor, prostrating himself before God. In fact, Augustine said it looked like he had been forcibly knocked down. (Perhaps the power of God fell on him!)

The man began to pray, Augustine said, with great earnestness, emotion, a flood of tears, and agitation of his whole body. Augustine meant that the man's whole body was shaking with sobs. It reminds us of what is said in the fifth chapter of James: *"The effectual fervent prayer of a righteous man availeth much"* (v. 16).

Augustine admitted, "For my part I could not pray. This alone, inwardly and briefly, I said: 'Lord what prayers of thy children wilt Thou ever grant if Thou grant not these?' For nothing seemed more probable than that he should die praying."

Augustine concluded by saying that when the man's surgeons came to remove the dressing, they found his diseased tissues perfectly healed.

This Carthaginian nobleman had simply turned his face to the wall and had found there is a God with whom nothing is impossible.

Dr. Yeomans relates how Martin Luther, too, knew what it was to turn his face to the wall "in utter despair of all human aid." One of Luther's helpers in the Protestant Reformation became seriously ill, and Luther went to see him. He found him near death.

Dr. Yeomans wrote, "Luther turned away from the awful scene to the window, and there called on God, urging upon Him all the promises he could repeat from the Scriptures, and adding, with incredible boldness that God must hear and answer now if He would ever have the petitioner trust Him again."

Think about this — a Lutheran minister prayed like this. Luther said, "I called on God. I called on God with all the promises I could repeat from the Scripture." In other words, Luther reminded God of every promise he could think of, and then with incredible boldness said, "God, You must hear and answer, because if You don't hear me, I won't ever be able to trust You again."

That's pretty bold, isn't it? That wasn't some wild-eyed Pentecostal preacher praying; that was a Lutheran!

Later, his friend wrote, "I should have been a dead man had I not been recalled from death itself by the coming of Luther." He was raised up. Luther wrote friends, "Philip is very well . . . I found him dead but by an evident miracle of God he lives."

What did Luther do? He turned his face to the wall. He saw nothing but God. He refused to see anything else. At first glance, his friend seemed virtually dead — but Luther didn't look at that. He turned and looked out the window.

He didn't see any houses. He didn't see any trees. He was looking at God. He was looking unto the God with whom all things are possible.

Think about what he said, "I reminded Him of all the promises I could think of, and then I said, 'Lord, if you don't hear me, I won't ever be able to trust you any more.' "

[1] From Lilian B. Yeomans, M.D., *The Great Physician.* Copyright © 1961, Gospel Publishing House. Reprinted by permission.

Chapter 3
Plead Your Case

Charles G. Finney said, "Argumentative prayers are the best kind of praying." Of course, Finney would say that because he was a lawyer. Finney was very argumentative.

Looking at the 43rd chapter of Isaiah, we see something God says:

ISAIAH 43:25,26
25 I, even I, am he that blotteth out thy transgressions for mine own sake, and will not remember thy sins.
26 Put me in remembrance: let us plead together: declare thou, that thou mayest be justified.

That's exactly what Luther did without even knowing it. *He repeated all the promises of Scripture he could remember where God promised to answer prayer.* He reminded God of them. *"Put me in remembrance,"* God said; *"let us plead together."* In other words, God is telling us to plead our case to Him!

Verse 26 continues, *"Declare thou, that thou mayest be justified . . . ."* That's from the King James translation. Another translation reads, "Set forth your cause that you might be justified."

The reason we don't get more results is because: (1) We don't turn our face to the wall and look to God and God alone; (2) Our praying is not intense enough. *"The effectual fervent prayer of a righteous man availeth much."* God said to Hezekiah, "I have heard your prayer. I have seen your tears."

If we're not careful, prayer can become just a form with

13

us. And even while we're praying, instead of turning our face to the wall, we're still looking at the impossibility of the situation. We're still trying to figure out how God can do it. Don't you figure out how God can do it. Let Him do it.

I remember years ago when word came that my mother, who was only 68 years old at the time, was dying. I went to the Lord. I turned my face to the wall. I turned away from everything else. With great intensity, I began to call upon Him.

Finally I said, "Now, Lord, You have promised us in your Word at least 70 or 80 years. That's a minimum. You said in your Word, 'I will satisfy you with long life.' "

(If you're not satisfied with 70 or 80 years, go on living beyond that.)

I said, "You promised us that 70 or 80 would be a minimum, and Momma's only 68. If she doesn't get the minimum, I'll never be satisfied. The longest day I live on this earth, I'm going to remind You of it. I don't mean I'm going to turn my back on You, but I'll never feel good toward You about it."

The Lord said to me immediately, just as plain as if He had been standing beside me — "All right. I'll do whatever you say about it."

I said, "Give her at least 80 years." I knew she didn't have enough faith to claim it on her own, but she lived to be 80. Just a few days after she passed her 80th birthday, she went home to be with the Lord.

I think sometimes we're too mealy-mouthed when it comes to seeking God.

Jesus said something about this subject: *"the kingdom of heaven suffereth violence, and the violent take it by force"* (Matt. 11:12).

God's the same God now He was then. He's the same
God King Hezekiah prayed to. He's the same God Martin
Luther prayed to. He hasn't changed. He's the God of the
ages. He is the Ageless One. With Him there is no shadow
of turning.

Thank God for this hour in which you and I live. Think
about it: We can read the Word of God. We can read
history. We can see what God is doing today in this char-
ismatic move.

How much stronger our faith should be. How much
more should we be encouraged through faith to take
authority over all the powers of hell and the devil.

We can turn our face to the wall, so to speak, pray to
God, and believe God, because we are workers with Him.
How do we know we are workers together? We know be-
cause the Word says so.

God has made man's cooperation necessary in the Plan
of Redemption. We must cooperate with God in order to
enjoy our rights in His redemptive plan. That's the reason
He said, *"If thou canst believe, all things are possible to him
that believeth"* (Mark 9:23).

The Bible tells us, *"the eyes of the Lord run to and fro
throughout the whole earth, to shew himself strong in the
behalf of them whose heart is perfect toward him"* (2 Chron.
16:9).

He sent His Word to tell us what His plan is. He sent
His Word to tell us that the Lord Jesus came and consum-
mated that plan, arose from the dead, and then sat down at
the right hand of the Father. You don't sit down until the
job is finished; that's why He sat down. He had finished the
job God sent Him to do. The Plan of Redemption is finished. Now it's up to us to believe it; it's up to us to
cooperate with Him.

That's the reason Jesus said, *"Go ye into all the world, and preach the gospel to every creature"* (Mark 16:15). Go tell them the Good News that Jesus bore their sins.

But that's not all the Gospel: *"Himself took our infirmities, and bare our sicknesses"* (Matt. 8:17).

Jesus wants us to go tell people that we are free from the bondage of Satan. That's what He said to the woman who was bent over, suffering from a spirit of infirmity: *"Ought not this woman, being a daughter of Abraham, whom Satan hath bound, lo, these eighteen years, be loosed from this bond on the sabbath day?"* (Luke 13:16). It was certain that Satan had bound her.

Hallelujah, I'm not in bondage to Satan! I'm not in bondage to sin! I'm not in bondage to sickness! I'm not in bondage to bad habits! I'm free! Jesus has set me free! *"And ye shall know the truth, and the truth shall make you free"* (John 8:32).

Chapter 4
Correct Your Situation

Paul, writing to the churches in Galatia, said, "Stand fast." We need to realize there's a God-ward side and a man-ward side to every battle, every victory. It isn't all God, and it isn't all you. You can see that in Hezekiah's case.

God had His part to play. He said, "Isaiah, go tell King Hezekiah to set his house in order, for under the present circumstances he shall die and not live."

Somebody will ask, "Did God change His mind?" No, God wanted to bless Hezekiah all the time, but He couldn't do any more for him than what He was doing under those circumstances. Hezekiah had a part to play, too. Notice even Isaiah couldn't do it for him.

Often we're looking for the prophet or the preacher to do it for us, but Isaiah did not change the situation. It was not Isaiah's prayer that changed the situation — it was Hezekiah's prayer!

Hezekiah was the only one who could do something about his situation.

It was Hezekiah who turned his face to the wall.

It was Hezekiah who prayed to God.

It was Hezekiah who "wept sore."

It was Hezekiah who changed.

Now God could do something for him. Now God could answer his prayer.

Isaiah hadn't gotten out of the courtyard before God told him, "Go back and tell Hezekiah, 'I've heard your prayers. I've seen your tears. And I'm going to add 15 years to your life.' "

Study what Hezekiah did. What worked for him will work for you, because God is the same God.

People who haven't studied the Bible would read this story and say, "Look at the inconsistencies in the Bible. Here it says he's going to die and here it says he's going to live. So God lied, didn't He?"

Just picking out verses and not reading them in context does not give you the whole picture. When you read this whole story, you understand what God is saying.

It wasn't the will of God for Hezekiah to die. God wanted the king to have His blessings. It was Hezekiah who stood in the way of God's blessings. When he corrected that situation, God could bless him.

Very often God will tell you what's going to happen under present circumstances — as He did Hezekiah — and you can change it. YOU can change it. Hezekiah did.

Too often we're looking for somebody else to do it for us. In teaching on faith, we bring out the fact that sometimes you can carry baby Christians on your faith. But you can only do that for a while. Usually people are going to have to receive help on their own, and *no one will receive permanent help without developing his or her own faith and prayer life.*

I've seen people healed, delivered, and even raised up from a deathbed through supernatural manifestations of the gifts of the Holy Spirit in my own or other people's ministries. But I've seen those same people one year, two years, or five years later, and the same disease, or something worse, had come back on them. And I've heard God say to me, "They're going to die." Under those circumstances, such as Hezekiah's circumstances, they were going to die.

Some of them didn't do a thing about it. They went ahead and died. (That doesn't mean they didn't go to heaven if they were believers.) But others, thank God, did something about it. Medical science said they were going to die. Yet *they turned their faces to the wall*. They prayed.

I prayed for my mother. I could do this for her because she was a baby Christian. All she had ever heard preached is that Jesus saves. She had only heard me preach two or three times. Later on, she heard me quite a bit on the radio, her faith began to develop, and she began to get answers for herself.

But at the time she was so ill, I knew she was a baby Christian and wouldn't be able to get healing for herself. That's the reason I jumped right in the middle of it and got results. If she had been more knowledgeable in God's Word, it would have been impossible for me to have done that for her.

I remember a dear Methodist woman whose husband was an educator in New York State. The doctors discovered she had a rare incurable disease. Only seven or eight people in the history of medicine had ever had it. Although the disease wouldn't kill her immediately, there was no cure, and the doctors said she would be dead within 10 years.

Somebody told this woman about the great meetings Kathryn Kuhlman was conducting, so she went to one. After Miss Kuhlman preached, she turned and looked right in this woman's direction. She did it by divine revelation.

Miss Kuhlman said, "There's a woman over here in this section who has an incurable disease. Doctors have told her only seven or eight people in the history of medical science have ever had it." Miss Kuhlman then named the disease.

The woman said, "I knew that was me. I went down there, she laid hands on me, and I fell under the power. When I returned to my doctors in New York City for my three-month checkup, they couldn't find a trace of the disease. It had all disappeared." The woman was healed — but not on her own faith, because she didn't know how to believe God.

She was like those people waiting for the troubling of the waters at the pool of Bethesda in the fifth chapter of John's Gospel. (When the angel troubled the water, the first person in got healed.) She went to Miss Kuhlman's service like that — just waiting for the intervention of divine sovereignty. And God works that way sometimes.

Three years passed. The woman and her husband were baptized in the Holy Spirit through the Full Gospel Business Men's Fellowship. She came to one of my meetings and said to my wife and me, "Brother and Sister Hagin, I haven't divulged this to my husband, but all the symptoms have come back on me. In fact, I am worse than I ever was before. Can you help me?"

I said, "Yes, I can. Come to the day teaching services if you can." (I was in Upper New York State for about six weeks, going from place to place.)

So she and some friends followed us from place to place. I remember before the six weeks were up, she came and said, "Brother Hagin, I want you and Sister Hagin to know that all my symptoms have disappeared. And I got it this time on my own faith. I know how I got it, and I know how to keep it!"

Chapter 5
A Favorite of the Father

You're not going to receive any final deliverance or help without developing your own faith and your own prayer life.

That's the reason I'm teaching as I am. I want you to turn your face to the wall. I want you to call upon God. He will hear you. Praise God, He loves you. God doesn't love one person any more or any less than He loves another person, because He's no respecter of persons (Acts 10:34).

Many times people think, *God will hear Brother Hagin pray, but He won't hear me*. But he will. He doesn't like me any better than He does you. Did you know that? He loves you just as much as He does me. He will hear your prayer just as quickly as He will mine. And He will answer your prayer just as quickly as He will mine. Yes, He will. He's your God just as much as He's my God.

God doesn't belong to me any more than He belongs to you. God doesn't have any favorites.

People should not do it, but I've seen people who have favorite children or grandchildren. A grandparent may give all his or her attention to this one child, excluding the others. This creates confusion and problems. It turns relatives away from one another.

But I want you to know that God doesn't have any favorite children, hallelujah. Every one of us is His favorite! I want you to know you're a favorite of His, glory to God, because of Jesus.

Here's a confession for you to repeat out loud:

I am a child of God.
He is my Father.
He is my very own Father.
I am His very own child.
I am a favorite with my Father.
We are all favorites with Him.
He loves every one of us with the same love.
He will hear every one of us pray.
My Father loves me.
My Father hears me when I pray.
My Father answers.
Oh, hallelujah, He is my Father.
He is my God.
Jesus is my Lord.
I am accepted in Jesus.

We preach and teach the Word of God from different directions, showing different methods of receiving healing, because it's all in the Word. Sometimes I think we talk about laying on of hands so much that people think that's all there is in the Bible. But no, that's just part of the biblical teaching on healing.

Nobody laid hands on Hezekiah. As far as I know, nobody even prayed for him!

From October 1979 through March 1982, I conducted daily Prayer and Healing School services on the RHEMA campus. However, I did not personally pray for people every day. Some days I would have our staff of healing instructors minister to the people.

One day a couple drove down from Missouri to attend the service. I was here and spoke, but I didn't lay hands on the sick that day. I asked the healing instructors to do it.

The woman was so disappointed. She went into a prayer

room, and one of our instructors taught her that only the Lord does the healing. The woman, however, was crying. Her feelings were hurt because Brother Hagin hadn't laid hands on her and prayed for her healing. And her husband was angry about it.

But the instructor prayed for the woman and cursed the massive tumor that was in her body. Afterwards, the couple drove back to Missouri.

Later the woman wrote and thanked the instructor. She said she had cried nearly all the way home — her husband was still mad — because Brother Hagin hadn't laid hands on her.

She had been scheduled for surgery. When she returned to her physician, the tumor had disappeared — and Brother Hagin didn't do it. So now the woman was very apologetic. Healing instructors, you see, have faith, too, praise God.

After all, the Bible doesn't say, "These signs shall follow Brother Hagin. He's the only one who will lay hands on the sick . . . ." No, "These signs shall follow THEM THAT BELIEVE."

We have had other cases of people who were healed through staff members' prayers. One young lady just 15 years old from Oklahoma City had a growth as large as a golf ball behind one of her eyes, and it was supposedly malignant.

An instructor laid hands on her. I read the letter the dear mother wrote back here to me personally, thanking me for having such nice instructors.

The girl's mother said that the instructor was so nice and gentle. He prayed with them and cursed the growth and commanded it to die. Then he prayed with the mother and she received the baptism in the Holy Spirit and spoke in other tongues.

When the mother took her daughter back to the doctor, he couldn't find the growth.

You see, Jesus is the Healer — not man.

Chapter 6
Act Like It's True

The Lord once told me to give people an opportunity to act on whatever I was teaching on — to act on the Word of God. That's what faith is — acting on God's Word — acting like it is true.

This is what I want you to do: Kneel if you can, or just bow your head and pray. Turn your face to the wall. Do you know what I mean by that now? Don't look at anything or anyone else. Don't look at Brother Hagin. Look to God and Him alone, the Eternal One. Turn your face to the wall. See Jesus only. See God with whom all things are possible. And then, blessed be God, cry out to Him. Pray out loud. Pray now.

Prayer:

Lord, You love me. Oh, thank You for your great love. Thank You for your great Plan of Redemption which You planned, dear Father, and sent the Lord Jesus to consummate.

Thank You, dear Father, because Jesus not only took our sins and bare our iniquities, but it is also written that He took our infirmities and bare our sicknesses. And what He bore, we do not need to bear. And because He bore them, we're free. We thank You for that today.

And on the basis of thy precious, holy, eternal Word, I receive my healing today. I believe. I believe thy Word.

I appropriate thy Word. I claim that Word. I take that Word as my own, because it belongs to me. You have no favorites. We are all your children. Blessed be the Name of the Lord.

25

I believe I receive healing today for my physical body, from the top of my head to the soles of my feet. Thank You, Lord Jesus.

I turn my face to the wall.

I turn away from man.

I turn away from all the symptoms.

I turn away from all the suffering.

I turn away from everything that tells me it is not so.

I look only to Thee.

Thou art the Eternal One. Thou hast declared it to be the truth. Thy Word is true, and I receive even now.

I thank You for my healing today, O Lord. I thank You for the very life of God that is in me and that is being made manifest in me even now. In the Name of the Lord Jesus Christ of Nazareth.

We call unto Thee. Thou hast heard us. Thou dost hear us. We appropriate thy Word. Forever, O Lord, thy Word is settled in heaven. We appropriate thy Word unto ourselves today. In the Name of the Lord Jesus Christ.

We thank You today. We praise You this day. We worship You this day. We magnify the Name of the Lord. Forever, O Lord, thy Word is settled in heaven. Blessed be the Name of the Lord.

Glory, reverence, and honor be unto Him, both now and forevermore. Jesus is the Name of the Lord.